VOLUME 1 | STEPS 1-12

12

Step

Poetry

Anonymous

Wild Rising Press
EVERGREEN, COLORADO

Published by Wild Rising Press

Editor: Judyth Hill
Book & Cover Design: Mary M. Meade
Red Phoenix: iStock.com/daikokuebisu

ISBN 978-1-957468-16-7

12

Step

Poetry

CONTENTS

PART 2

PART 3

PART 4

PART 5

Preface

A single writer penned these poems with humble intent to convey spiritual experiences in the language of the heart. To say each poem was written by a different person also rings true, because with each step my metaphysical self was being miraculously transformed.

> *When a man or a woman has a spiritual awakening, the most important meaning of it is that he has now become able to do, feel, and believe that which he could not do before on his unaided strength and resources alone. He has been granted a gift which amounts to a new state of consciousness and being.*
>
> ~Alcoholics Anonymous

I offer my experience with a prayer that it will afford strength and hope to those I would serve… you, dear readers.

—In honor of my chosen traditions, I remain,
Your anonymous lover

(The angels said) that they picture wisdom…
as a magnificent and highly ornate palace into
which one mounts by twelve steps.

—EMMANUEL SWEDENBORG

I Pray

with faithful trust
for divine inspiration and illumination
to awaken creative wisdom
from within
to my fingertips
where feral words fly
to roost in formations
on blank white pages
crows on winter snow
shadows of ravens

We admitted we were powerless over our destructive tendencies and that, when we followed them, *our lives became unmanageable.*

—GRANT R. SCHNARR

Step 1

Came to believe that a Power greater than ourselves could restore us to sanity.

—ALCOHOLICS ANONYMOUS

Step 2

Made a decision to turn our will and our lives over to the care of God as we understood God.

—CO-DEPENDENTS ANONYMOUS

Step 3

Bottom

I woke while asleep
in a lucid dream
to find I had lost
life's meaning.

Whatever that means!

See what I mean?

I circled 'round
spiraling down
battling myself
in a fight for survival.

I needed revival!

Not in a tent
rolling on the floor
like a peanut
in barroom sawdust.

Could I find relief
in a change of scene?
Fresh air to breathe?

Ha! Involuntarily
breath commanded trust.

Natural Grace

The winds of grace blow all the time.
All we need do is set our sails.

~SRI RAMAKRISHNA

I went on holiday
to a tropical paradise
where in the Sun I lazed
staring at my idle hands
all the long hot day.

My tired eyes closed,
I must have dozed.
Earthen colors blurred below
as I shared sight
with a raven in flight.

The breeze shifted east.
Roused to my feet,
all senses ripened,
I wandered in wonder
the heavenly island.

I smelled roots underground,
tasted mystery undersea.
I saw with clarity
in Father Sun's light,
felt satin air nuzzling me.

I heard divinity
in the songs of birds.
I knew myself to be
a sacred design
of cosmic harmony.

A thousand-petaled lotus
blossomed overhead
pouring violet rain.
My knees kissed Earth,
my palms met in prayer.

Though somehow renewed,
my anxiety bloomed
with afternoon shadows
as all that I knew
began fading from view.

I knew only one truth:
I revolve and rotate
with Mother Earth;
Father Sun stays
in just the same place.

Heart of Time

Mother Earth pirouettes,
slow dancing 'round Father Sun
attuned to cosmic vibrations
of unstruck sound in air,
beyond the sensory realm.
Dawn breaks through imagination.

Angelic time flies,
star-shaped blinding light,
flatlining in purgatory
where souls manifest
mortal bodies of flesh
to learn the circle story.

Powerless

When I took to my bed
for nighttime rest
each pink pound
of sunbaked flesh
screamed in agony.

Though weary of wakefulness
I feared more the mysterious
themes of my dreams
from the unseen reality
without boundary.

Seeking escape
from this rock and hard place
I gazed at the scene
outside the French doors
of my chamber of horrors.

There the lava mountain rose
dark against the sky.
The full moon shone
a path of gold on the sea
directly toward me!

Illusion or reality?

The magic light followed me
as I paced about the room.
My confusion grew
and drew me to the balcony.

Endless sky
roused endless fear.
Hopeless despair
flowed with my tears.
"Let me die!" I cried.

From the Milky Way
a shooting star flew to Earth
and struck me in the head!

I staggered back to bed
in complete defeat.
Blinded by the light
at last I could see
that I become powerless
when I choose to appease
my innate dark tendencies.

Lover's Leap

Willing to be willing
beget the energy
that carried me unwittingly
to a foreign space
of hopeful faith.
How do I choose light?
With principles placed
before personalities
and self-created deities,
the answer came to me,
...when feeling out of sight
For the ends of being
and ideal grace.
with the very sweetest
of all states of being.
Where love rules,
there is no will to power.
God is love.

Power of Choice

When that which is perfect has come,
that which is in part will be done away...
And now abide faith, hope, love, these three;
but the greatest of these is love.

~1 CORINTHIANS 13:10-133

Oh, that Love would Master me!
Inspire all I feel that feeds
thought and word and deed
of habit-hardened character,
govern every present moment
always and forever.
Quoth the Raven, So be it.

Storm Surge

*The ego on some level knows. It knows that
what is happening has to happen.
It knows that its personal desires have to be
sacrificed to the transpersonal.
It knows it is confronting death.*

~MARION WOODMAN

In a pulsed pattern of release
grief seeks its seasonal habitat
in the floodplain of my heartscape,
eroding ancient karmic paths.

After the bloodied waters recede,
pooling to rest in burial ground,
the Sun bakes reshaped terrain
of Love gone to seed in birth canals.

In Avila

clouds flying like birds
shape-shifting shadows on Earth
doubt seeks survival

tints, tones, shades of gray,
pearl, peek-a-boo powder blue
stormy sea of hope

PART 2

Made a searching and fearless moral inventory of ourselves.

Step 4

—ALCOHOLICS ANONYMOUS

Admitted to God, to ourselves and to another human being the exact nature of our wrongs.

Step 5

—ALCOHOLICS ANONYMOUS

Awareness Without Judgment

*When an inner situation is not made conscious, it
happens outside, as fate.*

~C.G. JUNG

*The problem with ego consciousness is this: believing
that it is the final reality, the ego process stops and does
not continue in its evolution. The technical term for this
process is called ignorance. Ignorance is the cause
of all suffering.*

~GOSWAMI KRIYANANDA

*Attachment is a state of ignorance based on a
memory of pleasure.*

~PATANJALI

I prayed to be fearless
I prayed to be thorough
to take a *searching*
moral inventory
of the motives in my story.

I prayed for illumination
and rigorous honesty to see
when attachment to the passion
of desire conjured fear,

Love's thieving enemy,
that blocks acceptance
with a wall of resentment.

I prayed to complete
my balance sheet
with hopeful vision to see
when Love's inspiration
allowed me to be
aligned with the Divine
in balanced harmony,
as Love intends for me.

I couldn't find a journal
nor a writing pen.
Dirty dishes needed washing,
clothes awaited laundering.
How did my butt end
up on my desk chair?
Who opened a blank
document on my laptop?

I focused on my fingers,
hunting and pecking
letters, words, paragraphs,
pages, pages, pages.

Illusions shattered silently
in dissipating fog.

I let them flow away
with tears of pain and joy.

My third step choice
to let go and let God
powered my fourth step—
it sure wasn't me!

Garbage In, Garbage Out

*Though one's confession was made to a human being,
he or she was chosen by the penitent for qualities of
true priestliness—holiness, wisdom, generosity, loyalty
and courage... So one did not necessarily choose one's
"priest" from among ordained professionals...
One looked for an anam chara, a soul-friend, someone to
be trusted over a whole lifetime.*

~THOMAS CAHILL

Within the confession
of all my transgressions
snaked a common thread.

I placed myself
above all else,
casting ego's shadow
across the path of Love
with behavior bred in vain
trying to survive
self-created pain.

I called my spirit back
from fears and negativity
of my wayward past.

I beseeched forgiveness;
I learned to forgive.

Love granted courage
allowing the virtues
of honesty and humility
to immerse me
in vulnerable intimacy.

Sun Center

stretching without haste
out of neglect in dissociation
deeper than sleep
wisdom danced in a dream
balanced on beams
of blue-violet vibration
conscious of inner connections
at conception's innocence
interconnected in Oneness
to awaken in a spiraling rise
galloping palomino passion
bareback and wild

PART 3

Were entirely ready to have God remove all these defects of character.

Step 6

—ALCOHOLICS ANONYMOUS

Humbly asked God to remove our shortcomings.

Step 7

—ALCOHOLICS ANONYMOUS

Entirely Ready

*Pondering in the heart is not a sentimental journey to the
Goddess. Pondering in the heart
involves the joy and the agony of consciously allowing
our own I am to magnify the great I AM.*

~ Marion Woodman

I woke while asleep
in a lucid dream
hearing stories told
of enlightened Yogis
who walk on charcoals.

The stench of burnt flesh
sickened my nose.
I sensed part of me
that I could not see
was burning to death!

Then I saw flames—
within them a rose.
As each petal opened
water poured forth
and I was awakened.

As Above, So Below

What hummingbird hovers at my heart?
Single note song unattached to storyline,
fury of kinetic energy poised outside
brittle walls of splintered shards defending
steady drumbeats of fearful history.

I sense sudden flight faster than my eye
can identify feathered shape or color.
Nectar circulates in my veins
attracting all for which I supplicate
while faith commands solitary waiting.

Light-years from here and now, stars implode
birthing black holes in outer space chaos.
Persephone's dark memories surprise
Earth's tectonic plates with a jolt
shifting well-worn handholds out of sight.

In suspended animation, I fall
to pieces—molecules of theta wave
alchemy in wisdom's timeless playground.
Unseen clouds of unknowable things
rain blessings from their pregnant bellies.

Pie-faced Moon mirrors Father Sun.
Oppositional resistance conceives
attraction of commonalities.
Prenatal, postnatal energies
combine, harmonizing heartstrings.

Unseen in New Moon darkness,
Pele strikes flint on stone, ignites unstruck
sound within my breast. Oh! Joyous chorus!

Dawn of Humility

I woke while asleep
in a lucid dream
heaven-bound mountain
blue lagoon womb of sea
Love surrounding me
pouring in, pouring out of me
paired within the heart of me
whole within the soul of me
to be
in Love.
Quoth the Raven, Forevermore.

PART 4

Made a list of all persons we had harmed and became willing to make amends to them all.

Step 8

—ALCOHOLICS ANONYMOUS

Made direct amends to such people wherever possible, except when to do so would injure them or others.

Step 9

—ALCOHOLICS ANONYMOUS

Amendment Mountain

Sweat years of tears
caked mud on my feet
as I shoveled deep
to unearth the list
of all those harmed
by my self-centeredness.
Sunbaked clay crumbled
into dust of willingness.
Attitude adjusted.
Angelic wings surprised me up
to mountainous terrain
where cold clear lakes
are fed by streams rushing
to refresh the reflection
of my unburdened soul.
I am free to go to those
from whom I seek forgiveness
so climbing I shall go.
Hi Ho!
Hi Ho!
Climbing I shall go!

Restitution

I love you.
I was wrong.
Please forgive me.
Thank you.

Spiders weave repairs
to rents in the web
of harmlessness.

Bees revise estimates,
raise production
of honey.

I rest
in restitution
of Oneness.

PART 5

Continued to take personal inventory and
when we were wrong, promptly
admitted it.

—ALCOHOLICS ANONYMOUS

Step 10

Sought through prayer and meditation to
improve our conscious contact with God
as we understood God, praying only for
God's will for us and the power to carry
that out.

—CO-DEPENDENTS ANONYMOUS

Step 11

Having had a spiritual awakening as the
result of these Steps, we tried to carry this
message to others and to practice these
principles in all our affairs.

—GRANT R. SCHNARR

Step 12

Accounting Department

Why, if it's possible to come into existence
as laurel, say, a little darker green
than other trees, with ripples edging each
leaf (like a wind, smiling): why then
do we have to be human, and keep
running from the fate
we are made for and long for?

~ RAINER MARIA RILKE

I woke while asleep
in a lucid dream
perched in a laurel tree
on Amendment Mountain
feeling appropriately
light as a butterfly
my conscience clear
as bright Sirius!
Father Sun laughed!
The mountain sang!
The laurel tree
clapped its hands!
Rattling me down
to the ground
with a chrysalis

quoting the poet:
Nothing wilts faster
than laurels that have
been rested upon.
~PERCY BYSSHE SHELLEY

Department of Repairs and Maintenance

In good orderly direction
sweeping, sweeping
keeping clean my street
sweeping, sweeping
keeping clean my street
paved with choices
sweeping, sweeping
litter of mistakes
keeping clean my street
sweeping, sweeping
keeping clean my street
sweeping my broom
right over your feet!
Sorry! Sorry!
Keeping clean my street
sweeping, sweeping
singing, singing
now I lay me down to sleep
in grateful peace

of emotional sobriety
relieved
of the bondage
of self.

I am that I am

I feel my body as my home.
I feel my body inwardly,
my home on Mother Earth,
surrendered to her gravity
flying 67,000 miles per hour
orbiting Father Sun.

Infinite space surrounds me,
a vessel of balanced energy
between Heaven and Earth,
right-sized consciousness,
stardust of Oneness.

Love surrounding me,
pouring in, pouring out of me—
pure manifestation
of infinite Light
unconditionally nourished
by infinite Life.

I am prayer,
shining in my place
in the Milky Way
no more, no less.

Rare Birds

Intention
Meditation

One hundred feathered prayers
winged to heaven from ashes
of mistakes no more repeated.

Intuition
Manifestation

Answers borne to Earth
on breath of angels bloomed
as joy to live in service.

Purification
Transformation

I see, I feel, I believe
beyond imagination's ken
vivifying divine will.

Now Love is mine
all the time.
Now all my Love is yours.

Let NOW Be Here.

Co-Creation

And acceptance is the answer to all my problems today.

~ALCOHOLICS ANONYMOUS

Acceptance allows being.
Activation allows becoming.
Acceptance and Activation with
Appreciation allow co-creation.

~MASTER MINGTONG GU

Gratitude

lives

in the Heart of Love

giving rise

to Love's spiral.

The path of my journey

within

narrows,

carries me higher

in a

dizzy dervish spin

of

Love, Joy and Wisdom.

Acknowledgments

PREFACE

Twelve Steps and Twelve Traditions, Alcoholics Anonymous World Services, Inc., 2013, p.106, 107.

Swedenborg, Emmanuel. "Angelic Wisdom Concerning Divine Providence."*Spiritual Recovery: A Twelve-Step Guide*, edited by Grant R. Schnarr, Swedenborg Foundation Publishers.

STEP 1

Spiritual Recovery: A Twelve-Step Guide, edited by Grant R. Schnarr, Swedenborg Foundation Publishers, p.253.

STEP 2

Alcoholics Anonymous. Alcoholics Anonymous World Services, 2001.

Lover's Leap: Browning, Elizabeth Barrett. "How Do I Love These? Let Me Count the Ways." *Sonnets from the Portuguese*, Mint Editions, Portland, 2022.

C.G. Jung, The Collected Works of C. G. Jung, Vol. 7: *Two Essays on Analytical Psychology*, April 1, 1972 by C.G. Jung (Author), Gerhard Adler (Translator), R. F.C. Hull (Translator)

God is love appears in: New King James Version. Thomas Nelson, 2020, 1 John 4:7-21 and: Sri Yogananda, P. (2014). *Autobiography of a Yogi*. Self-Realization Fellowship, 1946.

STEP 3

Co-Dependents Anonymous. Co-Dependents Anonymous, Inc., 2001.

Power of Choice: New King James Version. Thomas Nelson, 2020, 1 Corinthians 13:10-13.

Edgar Allan Poe, "The Raven," in The Complete Works of Edgar Allan Poe, ed. James A. Harrison (New York: Thomas Y. Crowell & Co., 1902), 212.

Storm Surge: Woodman, Marion. *The Pregnant Virgin: A Process of Psychological Transformation*. Inner City Books, 1985.

STEP 4 & 5

Alcoholics Anonymous. Alcoholics Anonymous World Services, 2001.

Awareness Without Judgment: Jung, Carl. *Christ: A Symbol of the Self*, Pages 70-71, para 126.

Kriyananda, Goswami. *The Spiritual Science of Kriya Yoga*. Temple of Kriya Yoga, 2002.

Patanjali, et al. Yoga Sutras. Parimal Publications, 1983.

Alcoholics Anonymous. Alcoholics Anonymous World Services, 2001.

Garbage In, Garbage Out: Cahill, Thomas. *How the Irish Saved Civilization: The Untold Story of Ireland's Heroic Role from the Fall of Rome to the Rise of Medieval Europe*. Knopf Doubleday Publishing Group, 1996.

STEP 6 & 7

Alcoholics Anonymous. Alcoholics Anonymous World Services, 2001.

Entirely Ready: Woodman, Marion. *The Pregnant Virgin: A Process of Psychological Transformation*. Inner City Books, 1985.

Dawn of Humility: Edgar Allan Poe, "The Raven," in *The Complete Works of Edgar Allan Poe,* ed. James A. Harrison (New York: Thomas Y. Crowell & Co., 1902), 212.

STEP 8 & 9

Alcoholics Anonymous. Alcoholics Anonymous World Services, 2001.

STEP 10

Alcoholics Anonymous. Alcoholics Anonymous World Services, 2001.

Accounting Department: Barrows, Anita, et al. *A Year with Rilke: Daily Readings from the Best of Rainer Maria Rilke.* HarperOne, 2009.

STEP 11

Co-Dependents Anonymous. Co-Dependents Anonymous, Inc., 2012.

STEP 12

Spiritual Recovery: A Twelve-Step Guide, edited by Grant R. Schnarr, Swedenborg Foundation Publishers.

Co-Creation: Alcoholics Anonymous. Alcoholics Anonymous World Services, 4th Edition, 2001.

Master Mingtong Gu, The Chi Center for Wisdom Healing Qigong, Galisteo, New Mexico.

The titles in this collection of 12 Step poems have been set in Bodoni 72, a modern interpretation by Alexander Tarbeev of the elegant Bodoni typeface designed by Giambattista Bodoni, the celebrated Italian typographer of the late 18th century.

Bodoni 72's contrasting thick and thin lines produce a "sparkling effect" on the page, announcing the enlivening effect of Stepwork, as embodied in these poems. The text has been set in Palatino, the universally admired work of noted typographer Hermann Zapf. Created in 1949 and based on the humanist types of the Italian Renaissance, which mirror the letters formed by a broad nib pen reflecting Zapf's expertise as a calligrapher. Palatino was designed to be particularly legible, but still give a sense of the hand of the author. Named after Giambattista Palatino, himself a master of calligraphy from the time of Leonardo da Vinci, this font lends the text a subtle remembrance and celebration of divinely supported individual effort.